Goal Achievement made simple

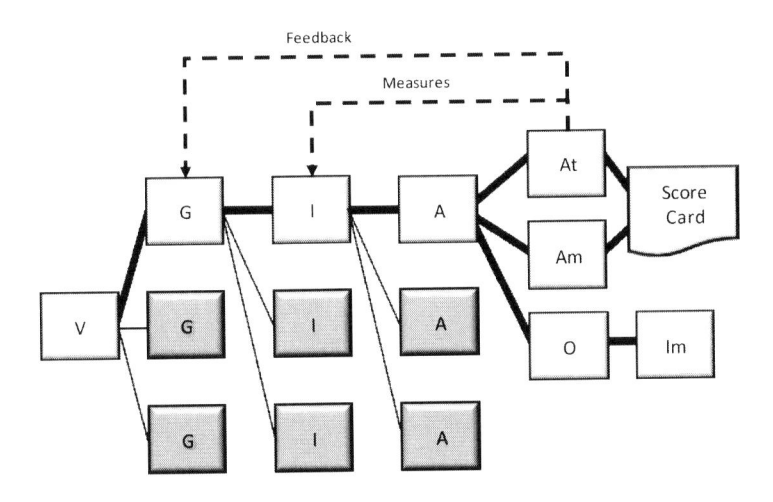

Stephen J. Thomas

RELIABILITY WEB.COM

Goal Achievement Made Simple
Stephen J. Thomas
ISBN 978-0-9838741-7-1
HF072012

© Copyright 2012 Reliabilityweb.com
Printed in the United States of America
All rights reserved.

This book, or any parts thereof may not be reproduced, stored in a retrieval system, or transmitted in any form without the permission of the publisher.

Opinions expressed in this book are solely the author's and do not necessarily reflect the views of the Publisher.

Publisher: Terrence O'Hanlon
Cover Design: Nicola Behr
Layout and Design: Sara Soto

For information address: Reliabilityweb.com
www.reliabilityweb.com
PO Box 60075 Ft. Myers, FL 33906
Toll Free: 888-575-1245 | Phone: 239-333-2500
Email: customerservice@reliabilityweb.com

10 9 8 7 6 5 4 3 2 1

Table of Contents

Introduction:	**Goal Achievement Made Simple**	1
Chapter 1	**Why Do Change Efforts Fail?**	5
Chapter 2	**You Can't Ignore the Culture**	13
Chapter 3	**Strategy in Support of Change**	21
Chapter 4	**The Goal Achievement Model**	27
Chapter 5	**Vision and Goals**	35
Chapter 6	**Initiatives**	39
Chapter 7	**Activities**	43
Chapter 8	**Measurement**	49
Chapter 9	**Outcomes and Impacts**	53
Chapter 10	**An Example of How It Works**	57
Chapter 11	**Sustainability**	63
Chapter 12	**The Beginning**	67
Bibliography		69
About the Author		71

Dedication

To Sophie Madeline Thomas
My granddaughter
Born June 3, 2011

Introduction
Goal Achievement Made Simple

Here is a question to ask yourself: Why do goals and the associated work tasks created by smart, dedicated people often fail to achieve the improvements for which they were developed? That question is often asked by managers and others within an organization who dedicated both their time and effort to see a task through to successful completion and obtain the value that was sought only to have it fail.

To make matters even worse, failures of this sort leave in their wake a disgruntled and frustrated workforce that is typically highly skeptical of investing their time and effort in the next initiative that comes along. After all, why bother? Their collective experience is that involvement is only going to be a waste of their time.

Believe it or not, the problem gets even worse! Assuming that more than one initiative has failed in this manner, failure becomes the norm and the organization begins evolving into one that expects failure and treats each new effort as simply "the program of the day." This generates the prevailing attitude that if we wait long enough, this effort, as those in the past, will pass into oblivion in short order. Organizations that have fallen into this mind set, and there are many, will have an extremely difficult time breaking this pattern for future efforts.

That's the bad news. The good news is the mental model of continuous failure can be broken. Organizations have the ability to break the mold and move forward. There is a very real possibility they can experience success and create a new mindset about change. A mindset where they will actually embrace new goals knowing full well there is a definitive and proven plan to achieve success.

The goal of this book is to provide you with an understanding of why task-based change seems to fail more times than not and present a process that reverses this course of behavior. This book will show you how to achieve your organization's vision and the related goals through the use of a tool called the Goal Achievement Model. Included in this book is a detailed description of the model, questions to make you think about this process as it relates to your organization and an example to show you how it can be utilized.

Most books simply provide information to get you started. This book not only gets you started, it accompanies you on your journey to successful implementation of your goals.

This book is divided into three parts. The first part is designed to provide you with an in-depth understanding of why change efforts fail. After all, if you don't understand the root cause of failure associated with change, how could you ever expect to change the process?

The second part introduces you to the Goal Achievement Model tool. It is a highly effective way to drive a wide-range of activities to successful completion, and as a result, accomplish your goals and ultimately the company's vision. You will also gain an understanding about the linkage between all of these components since this is a very important aspect of this process. Also in this section, I introduce you to goal achievement model measurement techniques that will enable you to keep track of the status of your overall effort right down to the activity level.

The third section, while shorter than the others, addresses a critical component – sustainability. Lack of a sustainability process often accounts for the failure of efforts that experience initial success but fail over time. There are many causes for sustainability breakdowns, some of which can be avoided, but others cannot. However, we will explore them all so you can recognize the importance of doing more than simply implementing change and expecting it to magically take hold.

There also is a series of questions at the end of each chapter that will enhance your understanding of the model and all that it embodies. The questions require some thought because they address your organization and how it approaches change. Examining how your company handles these efforts, along with an understanding of the model, should start you in the right direction. Take time to think through the questions and perform the activities. This effort will contribute to your understanding and improved use of the model.

Why Do Change Efforts Fail?

Change efforts fail as a result of issues that are both within our control and out of our control. This book focuses on the former rather than the latter since there is no need to dwell on things beyond our control other than to recognize them for what they are. For example, the sale of your company resulting in new management and a new way of doing things can, in a blink of an eye, render all your hard work of implementing a change effort useless. At times such as these, you may be able to retain some aspects of the effort, but ultimately a new owner with a new direction is going to make your efforts vanish. It is unfortunate that this happens, but it is an outcome of new ownership many, if not all of you reading this book, have experienced. These external agents of change are often enormously disruptive and one of the reasons why many successful efforts are replaced even before they have had an opportunity to show value.

What I want to address in this book are the things within your span of control. Change efforts that fail within a work environment that is not experiencing changes in its external conditions are what are important. Why? Because these failures don't have to occur! Firms that fit this model have initiatives in place, often extensively supported by the senior leadership team, that just fail to achieve a successful outcome either immediately or over time. A few examples are in order, many of which you may find familiar:

- A predictive or preventive maintenance program is developed, people trained and the effort deployed, only to fail as the organization can't seem to dislodge themselves from their existing "break it, fix it" mentality.

- An operator-driven reliability process is deployed, but the monitoring equipment seems to always break and the operators are always too busy to perform the designated tasks.
- A planning and scheduling process is put into place to improve the effectiveness and efficiency of the workforce, but the schedule is always set aside to address the emergencies of the day.

These examples are only a small sampling of the efforts that fail. And if you asked the organization, many would tell you these initiatives would have added real value if they had been successfully implemented.

So what is the problem? The answer is the organization viewed changes like those cited as tasks to be put into place and forgotten. They failed to view these efforts as part of something much bigger, designed to function not only at a tactical level, but be strategic in nature and fully aligned with the organization's vision and mission.

Before moving on, we need to take a moment and define some of these terms so we are all on the same page. There are five definitions that require a common understanding because they are used throughout this book. There are other terms as well, and they will be defined as we discuss them in the applicable chapters.

- **Vision** – A vision is "an idealized, collective picture of a future state which is integrated into the organization's culture. It is a stretch, yet achievable over an extended period of time with a great deal of work and collective focus." – Steve Thomas, *"Successfully Managing Change in Organizations."*

Additionally, it is an evolving process, so as the organization gets close to its attainment, the vision is evaluated and enhanced.

It is important that the vision creates the same picture for everyone; otherwise the organization runs the risk of vision disconnect as various groups with different pictures of the future of the company try to achieve them. Just think for a minute the confusion and misdirection a problem of this nature could create. For this reason, the vision must be short, easily understood and crystal clear.

- **Mission** (a term often confused with vision) – A mission statement is a description of the company's core values and purpose for being. In other words, the organization's reason for existence. The mission supports the vision as they work together.

Let's examine the interaction between these two terms. Suppose a company's vision is to be the number one manufacturer of a product "X" in the world. As an employee, this short statement serves to create a picture of the desired future state of the business. What's required to attain the vision is the mission statement; the expression of the core values of the firm. For our example, we will say that the company's mission is to operate the business in a safe, reliable and environmentally-sound condition with attention to optimal production. If the organization embraces this mission statement, then quite possibly the vision of its future is attainable. Not following the mission may still enable the company to be number one, but its core values would have been compromised.

Two other terms that require a common understanding are strategy and tactics. These two terms express vastly different modes of operation. In fact, they are mutually exclusive or, in other words, they cannot coexist. The reason is that strategic and tactical thinking takes place in different hemispheres of the brain and, unfortunately, these two hemispheres do not communicate with each other very well.

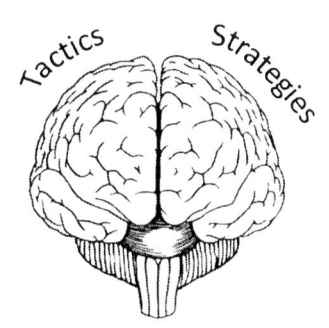

FIGURE 1 - STRATEGY AND TACTICS

- **Strategy** – This type of work addresses longer term efforts not focused on the day-to-day, but rather on the longer view. It deals with what needs to be accomplished over time to achieve the vision and mission that has been established.

- **Tactics** – This type of work deals directly with the day-to-day work of the organization. These are the specific work steps that are required to maintain the facility's operation. In the world of reliability and maintenance, this work is usually represented by the daily work schedule printed from the computerized maintenance management system or CMMS for short.

The important thing to understand is tasks need to be designed and implemented to achieve the strategy and the strategy to achieve the mission. They most certainly work hand-in-hand, but can't be done at the same time. Consider all the times when you were given a strategic task to complete while you handled the daily task-based activities associated with your job. How many of those strategic efforts actually were accomplished in conjunction with the daily tasks? Most likely, you did the work during off hours or at home when you had the time to engage the strategic part of your brain.

There is one more term that needs to be addressed; one which is most often misunderstood. That term is organizational culture. Were you ever told that "to improve we need to change our culture?" The follow-up question is, Did you understand what that really meant and how difficult it was going to be to accomplish? To help us on our journey to goal achievement, we need to define culture.

- **Culture** – "A pattern of shared basic assumptions that the group has learned as it solved its problems…that have worked well enough to be considered valid and, therefore, taught to new members as the correct way to perceive, think and feel in relation to those problems."– E. Schein *"Organizational Culture and Leadership."*

This is an important definition and the topic of culture will have a separate chapter dedicated to helping you see how this component is critical to a successful change effort.

With the above definitions in hand, let's return to the discussion of why change initiatives fail. They fail because organizations try to implement tasks independently of the culture and the elements that compose strategic thinking and action. In other words, the organization perceives a need, for example a machinery predictive maintenance program, and then goes about designing and implementing it while completely disregarding the existing culture and the strategic elements of change. Then as it fails either right away or over time, management scratches their collective heads and wonders why.

How does culture and strategy interact with the task-based changes you wish to implement? Figure 2 shows this relationship.

```
          /\
         /  \
        /Tasks\
       /------\
      / Strategic Elements \
     / "The Eight Elements of \
    /        Change"           \
   /----------------------------\
  /      Cultural Elements       \
 /   "The Four Elements of Culture"\
/_____\
```

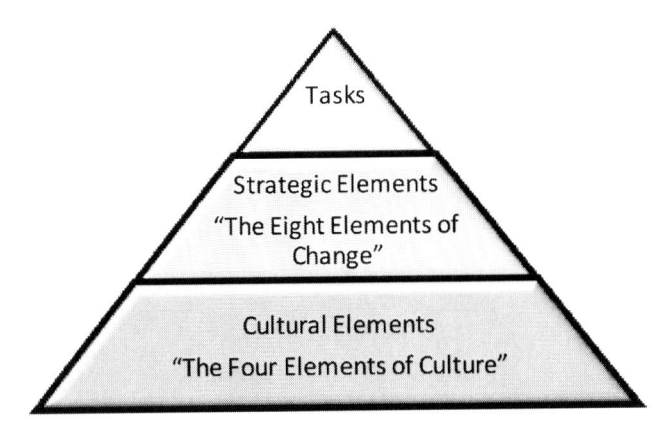

FIGURE 2 - THE RELATIONSHIP – CULTURE, STRATEGY AND TACTICS

The relationship is in the form of a pyramid, a change pyramid if you will. At the bottom are the elements of culture. They are the foundation of all that you do because if your strategy and resultant tasks are not aligned and supported by the culture, success will not be the result. There are four elements of culture and they will be discussed in Chapter 2. At the next level are the elements of strategy. There are eight of these and I will discuss them in detail in Chapter 3. Finally, after culture and strategy are firmly in place, only then can tactical efforts be deployed. The alternative is trying to support the top of the change pyramid without a solid base on which to build it. The results of building on a poor foundation are obvious and something we wish to avoid at all cost.

There are other reasons why change efforts fail, even if you understand and address the elements of culture and strategy. They are less obvious but are still significant and require some discussion.

First is what I refer to as the project mentality. The vast majority of reliability and maintenance professionals (this also includes technicians) are engineers, or through their on-the-job experiences and training, think like engineers. This logical process has everyone thinking about work initiatives as projects. A project is an effort that has a beginning and an end, at which point, hopefully, you pat yourself on the back for a job well done and move on to the next project in the queue. The change efforts we are discussing in this book are not projects! Of course they all have beginnings, but they do not have ends. The effort may change somewhat as you move from development to implementation to a sustainability mode, but there is no end. Change efforts fail when management treats them as projects and, after a time, refocus their efforts elsewhere leaving the effort to flounder and ultimately fail. That is not to say management can't refocus on other possibly more pressing matters, but it does say a sustainability and oversight process needs to be left in place to assure all of the work done to affect the change was not wasted. We will discuss sustainability in a later chapter.

The other less obvious cause of failure is to execute a task-based change, but not have a process in place to rigorously drive the detailed activities associated with the effort to completion. The other aspect of this part of the change process is devising provisions to not only sustain what has been put in place, but to provide a process to address continuous improvement.

Things to Think About & Things to Do

1. Identify one or two change efforts that have failed either initially or after a period of time.

    a. Describe why you feel they failed.

    b. What short-or long-term damage was done?

    c. How accepting do you feel the organization was the next time a new initiative was developed?

2. Describe an assignment where you were asked to perform tactical and strategic work at the same time.

    a. How well did that work for you?

    b. When did the real strategic work really take place – after hours, weekends?

3. Have you ever been involved in a maintenance initiative that was treated as a project?

    a. What happened when management decided that the project had reached its conclusion?

    b. What could have been done differently?

You Can't Ignore the Culture

At the base of the change pyramid shown in Figure 3 is organizational culture.

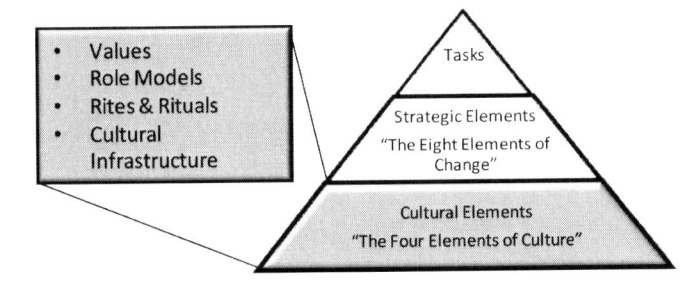

FIGURE 3 - THE FOUNDATION – CULTURE

Pyramid:
- Tasks
- Strategic Elements "The Eight Elements of Change"
- Cultural Elements "The Four Elements of Culture"
  - Values
  - Role Models
  - Rites & Rituals
  - Cultural Infrastructure

The definition at this point deserves to be restated.

- **Culture** – "A pattern of shared basic assumptions that the group has learned as it solved its problems…that have worked well enough to be considered valid and, therefore, taught to new members as the correct way to perceive, think and feel in relation to those problems." – E. Schein

Think about this definition in relationship to specific behaviors that take place in your organization and you will begin to realize how ingrained culture can be within an organization. These ingrained behaviors make change all that more difficult. For example, let's consider the culture of reactive maintenance; one that a great many organizations have found very difficult to alter. Consider this scenario:

The reliability of the plant is marginal at best, resulting in frequent breakdowns of the assets and, of course, the manufacturing process in which they operate. As a result, the maintenance staff is constantly working in the "break it, fix it" mode. In fact, they are so good at it that rapid repair is their recognized skill. Since they are able to repair breakdowns quickly, they are constantly receiving praise from production for "saving the day." The supervisors and engineers are recognized for their efforts through promotions and other forms of recognition by senior management. Over time, maintenance learns that this mode of operation is the expected norm. The department staffs its teams with rapid repair technicians, it doesn't plan its work because scheduling will only be interrupted by plant emergencies and the warehouse is overstocked with every part they may ever need so it is instantaneously available. As this mode of behavior continues, maintenance begins to think, perceive and believe that this is the best and only way work can be performed. After all, they are good at it and management reinforces their behavior. This mode of operation becomes their culture. Consider for a moment how difficult it would be for the company to change a culture such as this one to a new culture anchored in a preventive/predictive mode, a culture clearly contrary to the existing work culture and the organization's expressed values. Difficult is an understatement!

What I have just described is the first of four elements of culture – organizational values. To implement successful, long-lasting change, the values of an organization must be clearly understood and applied to drive the change. If they are not aligned with what you are trying to achieve, you are going to have a real problem. The example I just cited points that out rather well.

Besides organizational values, the other elements of culture are role models, rites and rituals, and cultural infrastructure. Each of these is extremely important in its own right, but when taken as a collective whole, they shape how the organization works. Consequently, if they are not aligned with what you are trying to implement, problems most certainly will occur.

Let's examine each of the elements of culture individually and then see how they work collectively to fashion an organization's culture. After doing so, we can then see what needs to be done to the culture to support the new changes that you wish to put into place.

- **Organizational Values** – A company's basic, collectively understood, universally applied and wholly accepted set of beliefs about how to behave within the context of the business. They describe what achieving success feels like. These values are internalized by everyone in the company and, therefore, are the standard for accepted behavior.

  The bottom line is the organization's values are what employees believe are the correct way to execute work. It is what they do without even thinking about it because they, collectively and individually, know that the behavior and action they are putting forth is correct. Remember the definition of culture – it is how they were taught to think, feel and act in relation to efforts that are required in order to operate and maintain the business. The effort needed to alter the value system, even slightly, points out the extreme difficulty one faces when trying to change the culture.

- **Role Models** – Individuals within a company who have been identified as successful are those we want to emulate so we can become successful as well. Consider your role models, those individuals who model successful behavior for you and others in your organization. There is little doubt that they exhibit the values that are part of the organization's culture in their everyday work. If they didn't, then there is a great likelihood they would not be as successful as they are.

  Now consider a company with a reactive repair value set. Those who are successful and have been recognized and rewarded accordingly are those who model and execute in the reactive repair mode. If you wish to change this mode of operation to one focused on asset reliability, these individuals will need to model a completely different behavior because, after all, these are the people that the new and upwardly mobile employees are copying. Making this change is not going to be easy since these individuals are currently recognized and promoted for performing in a very different way than what is being implemented in your reliability process.

- **Rites and Rituals** – These two terms describe the activities we perform and reward every day without even thinking about why we do them. Rituals are the things we do and the rites are how the organization recognizes and rewards behaviors that support the rituals, or punishes those who do not perform as directed. These are also ingrained in an organization's collective behavior and, as a consequence, extremely difficult to dislodge or change. A good example of this in the reactive world is how everything stops and the work is redirected when a plant emergency job (real or fabricated to get work accomplished) is called in by production. The actions of the workforce are immediate (rituals) and the rewards (rites) are provided for "saving the day."

- **Cultural Infrastructure** – The last of the four elements of culture is what is known as the cultural infrastructure. It is not really a single element, but rather a group of behaviors that an organization exhibits to maintain the status quo; in our case the existing culture. They include:

  ○ Storytellers – People within the organization who tell "war stories" typically in meetings or group gatherings. While these stories appear to be insignificant, they are not. What the storyteller is actually doing is relating in the form of a story what is and is not culturally accepted behavior.

  ○ Keepers of the Faith – These individuals are the organization's mentors; those who provide guidance either directly or indirectly as to how those being mentored should think, perceive and feel with relationship to the work they are performing.

  ○ Gossipers, Spies and Whisperers (in the boss' ear) – This collective grouping spread inaccurate, incomplete, or even confidential information that can seriously undermine a change initiative, causing delays and extensive damage control. By passing along such information, they fill communication voids and slow down the effort.

There are also aspects of the cultural infrastructure that are not actually people. These are symbols and language.

  ○ Symbols are things the organization does that help lock the existing culture in place. Examples include office space sized by job grade, other perks provided by job grade, and even things like designated parking and executive dining.

○ Language also tends to solidify the existing culture by differentiating groups by virtue of the language or acronyms they use in their daily dialogue. This eliminates others from membership since they don't understand the language. Departmental acronyms are a good example.

When taken all together, these four elements make it difficult to change a culture that has proven (or appeared to prove to the incumbents) to be successful. Figure 4 shows how the elements reinforce each other to essentially lock an existing culture in place.

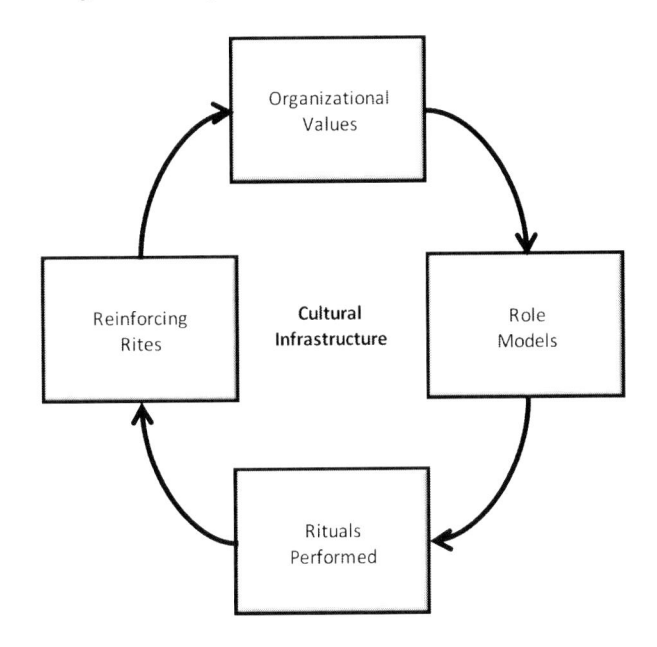

FIGURE 4 - THE FOUR ELEMENTS OF CULTURE REINFORCING LOOP

For instance, let's consider the reactive maintenance process. In our example, this process has not been altered because it supports and is part of the organization's values. As a result, people perform in compliance with the values and they are supported by the role models. Rituals are rewarded through the rites that reinforce the reactive behavior. The result is the existing culture is reinforced, continues and resists change.

So how do you change the culture? The answer is to alter the value system, which in turn creates new rituals, reinforcing rites and a new set of role models. Deciding to do this is one thing, doing it successfully is quite another. That is why we need to discuss and address the strategic elements of change in the next chapter.

Things to Think About & Things to Do

1. What is your organization's culture?
   a. What are the shared basic assumptions relating to reliability and maintenance?
   b. What is taught to new members as the correct way to think, perceive and feel about the work?
   c. Has the organization ever tried to change the values? If they were successful or unsuccessful, what do you think was the reason?

2. What are your organization's values? Is what is written the same as what is practiced? Is what is stated in sync with what is done?

3. Who are the role models in your company? Can you see how the behaviors they model reinforce the value system?

4. Identify some rituals and their reinforcing rites. How do they perpetuate the culture?

5. Think of a war story you may have heard and write down how it shows the expectations of the existing culture.

Strategy in Support of Change

- Leadership
- Work process
- Structure
- Learning
- Technology
- Communication
- Interrelationships
- Rewards

Tasks

Strategic Elements
"The Eight Elements of Change"

Cultural Elements
"The Four Elements of Culture"

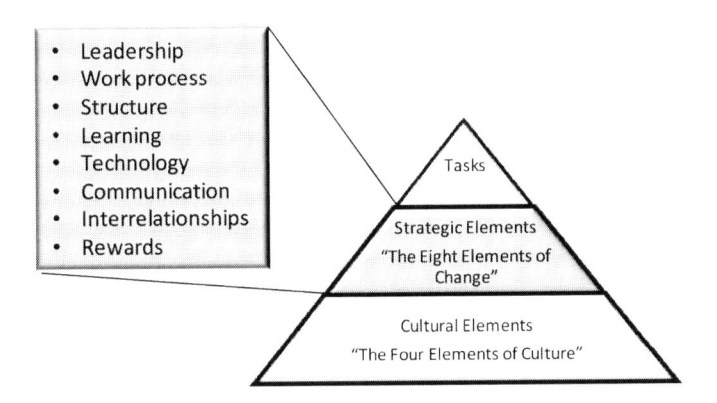

FIGURE 5 - THE STRATEGIC ELEMENTS OF CHANGE

Now let's discuss the strategic level of the change pyramid. Just as culture defines a company, strategy or the strategic elements are how the culture is continually reinforced and presented to the employees. It is the glue that ties the culture into successful task implementation. This is why culture supports strategy and, in turn, strategy supports tasks.

As previously mentioned, there are eight elements of change that need to be discussed and understood since they play a critical part in the change equation. They are:

- **Leadership** – For a change to take place, leadership is the key element. An organization will follow their leaders. In other words, those things the leader considers important will also be considered important by their subordinates. That is one reason why change or other efforts fail. As the leadership refocuses their attention away from an effort, so does the organization. For this reason, the leadership needs to recognize that the effort is not a project and at some level they need to maintain continual focus.

Not every leader is able to do this because these efforts are typically strategic in nature and the leader has a great many tactical issues to address every day. Plus, as we learned, tactical and strategic thinking do not coexist very well. Many leaders thrive in tactical situations. They are called transactional leaders. Others thrive in strategic situations and are called transitional leaders. Since both types can't function within the same individual at the same time (remember the issue about strategy and tactics), you need a leadership team with individuals responsible for each type of change – transactional and transitional.

- **Work Process** – The work processes are how things get accomplished. Work processes involve a number of steps, often executed by different departments or individuals to accomplish a task or set of tasks. In our case, we are going to be implementing change and this change brings with it new processes that need to be carefully crafted for the overall effort to be a success.

- **Structure** – Organizational structure supports the work processes. A reactive or proactive maintenance organization with the supporting processes will invariably look very different. Therefore, as you change your process, you need to alter, with great care, the structure to support it. The reason I specify "great care" is because you only want to make structural changes a few times. Multiple changes over a short time frame will lead many to think you have not clearly thought out what you wish to accomplish. This is also the time to properly position your new role models in the organization.

- **Group Learning** – As the change you have created is deployed, it is critical that those who are expected to perform differently have been trained to do so. The development of this training takes time and effort and needs to be started and ready long before the actual change is put into place.

There is a second aspect of group learning that also needs to be considered. In the world of change, nothing is ever 100% right the first time. For this reason, there needs to be a process in place whereby the organization learns from the things that worked well and also from the things that didn't work so well. Along with this should be a feedback process so what was learned along the way can be applied on a timely basis to further improvement.

- **Technology** – This element is not about the complex IT hardware and software that is used in your company. It is more specific; it addresses only the tools used to support the reliability and maintenance work processes. Many firms have failed to purchase and deploy the correct software and hardware necessary to support a reliability-focused effort. Others that have the technology may not have kept up with the recent releases or be using the tools they have correctly. In any case, a technology assessment is needed so the right technology is in place to support your change effort. Without the technology in place, the change effort will be seriously undermined.

- **Communication** – This element of change is critical! Without proper communication, there is chaos. Those in the organization will not understand what you are trying to accomplish and will ultimately fill the communication void with wrong or damaging information that leaves you with a great deal of wasted time in damage control.

    I can't say enough about the importance of this element. The communication needs to be up-front, accurate, timely, well thought out and delivered on a continuous basis. The goal has four components:

    ○ To explain what you are going to do as well as why and when

    ○ To describe how you are going to do it

    ○ To explain how you will keep everyone updated on the status (good or bad)

    ○ To solicit help and support from the organization in the form of involvement and feedback.

- **Interrelationships** – In industry, reliability maintenance, or for that matter any departmental function, cannot succeed in isolation.

That is why this element is so important. Everyone must understand the change that is taking place and be aligned behind the effort. Without positive interrelationships across departmental boundaries, problems will arise making the change effort difficult or even impossible to bring to a successful conclusion.

- **Rewards** – Last but not least are the rewards. Often when people think of rewards, the first thing that comes to mind is money. While financial gain is important, of greater importance for most is success of the enterprise and their ability to be part of that success. Certainly this type of success provides long-term employment and the sought after financial gain.

As you must recognize by now, each of these elements is of vital importance if you wish your change effort to be successful. However, as important as they are as independent elements, they are even more important as a collective group. Remove any one from the overall effort and the effort's success will be in jeopardy.

Figure 6 shows the relationship of the elements in the overall change process.

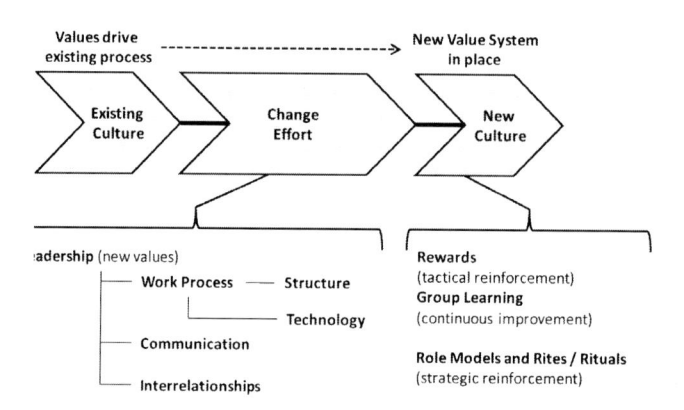

FIGURE 6 - THE ELEMENTS OF CHANGE IN THE OVERALL PROCESS

Of importance in the above diagram is the role played by the cultural and strategic elements of change – the supporting structures of the change pyramid. Consider, for example, the implementation of a highly focused planning and scheduling process into a culture that was totally reactive. Let's examine what would likely be the issues associated with a failure to apply the cultural or strategic elements to the change process. Figure 7 indicates the issues that would be apparent if elements were removed.

```
                    Tasks
              Strategic Elements
              "The Eight Elements of
                    Change"
              Cultural Elements
           "The Four Elements of Culture"
```

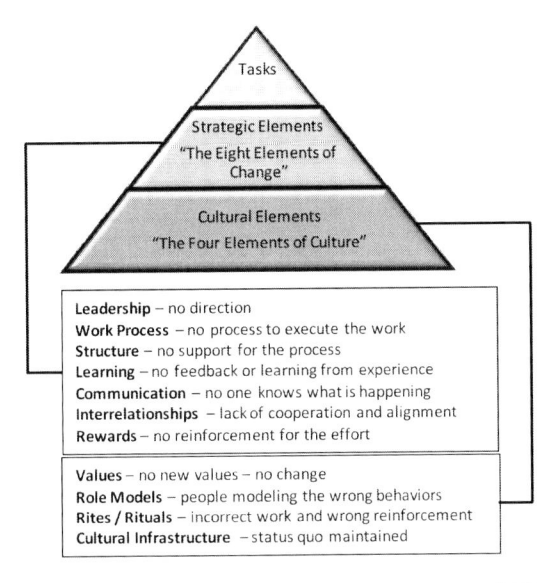

Leadership – no direction
Work Process – no process to execute the work
Structure – no support for the process
Learning – no feedback or learning from experience
Communication – no one knows what is happening
Interrelationships – lack of cooperation and alignment
Rewards – no reinforcement for the effort

Values – no new values – no change
Role Models – people modeling the wrong behaviors
Rites / Rituals – incorrect work and wrong reinforcement
Cultural Infrastructure – status quo maintained

FIGURE 7 - WHAT IF AN ELEMENT IS MISSING?

Obviously with one or more of the strategic or cultural elements missing, your change effort is going to suffer. The next chapter will describe the Goal Achievement Model, a tool you can use to avoid these problems.

Things to Think About & Things to Do

1. Have you ever experienced an effort that was working well until the leadership lost focus and no longer paid any attention to it? Describe it and think about what could have been done to avoid the problems that lack of focus caused.

2. Consider if the structure you have in place would support a major change to a different mode of operation for the reliability and maintenance function.

3. How well does communication take place in your plant/organization? Does the rumor mill the cultural infrastructure) have the information before the official channels? How much damage control is required due to inaccurate communication?

4. Do departmental interrelationships get in the way of progress? Why does this happen and what do you think should be done to improve it?

5. Take a successful and an unsuccessful change effort and determine how the eight elements of change and the four elements of culture contributed to its success or failure.

The Goal Achievement Model

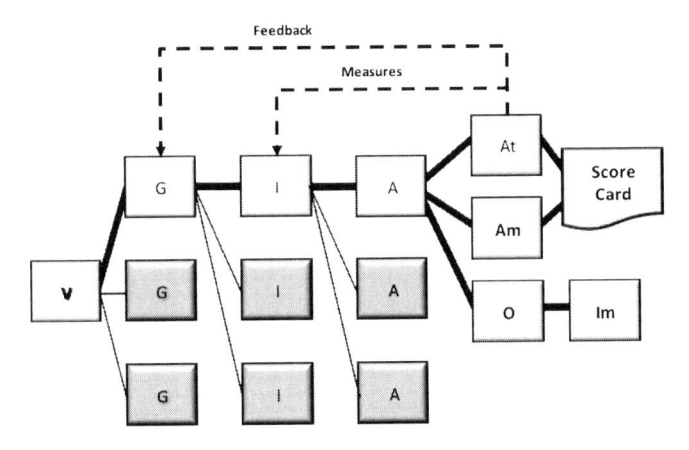

FIGURE 8 - THE FULL GOAL ACHIEVEMENT MODEL

This chapter focuses on a model you can use to achieve your firm's vision, goals, initiatives and activities. It is called the Goal Achievement Model and is the central element of this book. Use of the model should help you reverse the statistic that 80% of change efforts fail. The reason for the model's success lies in how it is constructed and used because it addresses far more than simple implementation of a task-focused change effort.

The value the Goal Achievement Model delivers are numerous:

- The use of the model creates universal understanding of the overall goals and how individuals can contribute to the effort.

- It provides a broad focus addressing the change effort at all levels of the organization.

- It links the vision and goals to specific initiatives and activities – the actual tasks that you are trying to accomplish.
- The model provides a tracking framework so you can measure completion of the various activities.
- It provides a feedback mechanism so goals can be periodically reviewed to assure that the effort is on track.
- It forces you to prioritize the vast number of initiatives and their related activities into a manageable effort, ensuring nothing gets lost along the way.
- It enables other departments, who may or may not have overlapping goals, to coordinate the total effort.
- It provides a good reporting tool upward to senior management, then through peers and the workforce. In this manner, everyone can see how they fit and can contribute.
- It provides an historical record of all activities (those that were done and those that were not) for future reference.
- It delivers an oversight tool so the process and its evolution can be tracked.

As you can see, the model provides a host of benefits that support and help drive your change effort to a successful outcome.

The balance of this chapter describes the model so you have a clear understanding of what it is about and how it functions. The following five chapters describe in detail the components and the sixth provides you with an example you can refer to as you undertake your own Goal Achievement Model effort.

Figure 9 portrays the Goal Achievement Model in its simplest form.

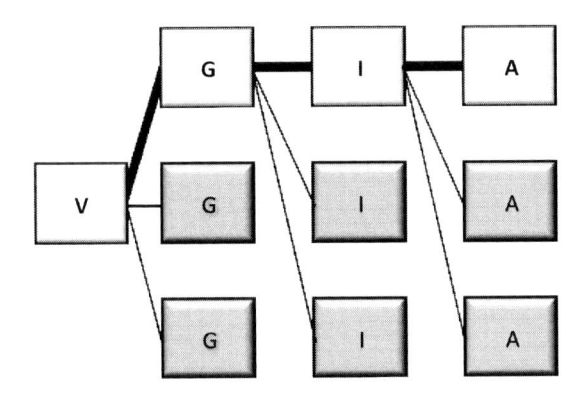

FIGURE 9 - THE GOAL ACHIEVEMENT MODEL – SIMPLEST FORM

In this model, there is a singular vision (V). Typically this is a corporate statement with implications that reach beyond just reliability and maintenance, but certainly one of which reliability and maintenance is an important part. The reliability and maintenance component of the vision is represented by the goals (G) that are created supporting the vision. Each goal is then supported by the initiatives (I). Just as there can be more than one goal, there certainly will be multiple initiatives. Each initiative then has specific activities (A) where the actual work identified is performed. There also will be more than one activity for each initiative.

The true value of the Goal Achievement Model is that everyone can see how the activities drive the initiatives, which in turn drive the goals that enable the vision to be achieved. This has immense impact since everyone within the organization can see how their activities contribute. Certainly this helps people engage, compared to different circumstances where they may not have chosen to get involved because they could not envision the relevancy of what they were doing. Further, if the linkages are not clear, the organization should consider questioning if the activities on which they are working are correct. This downward and upward relationship is shown in Figure 10.

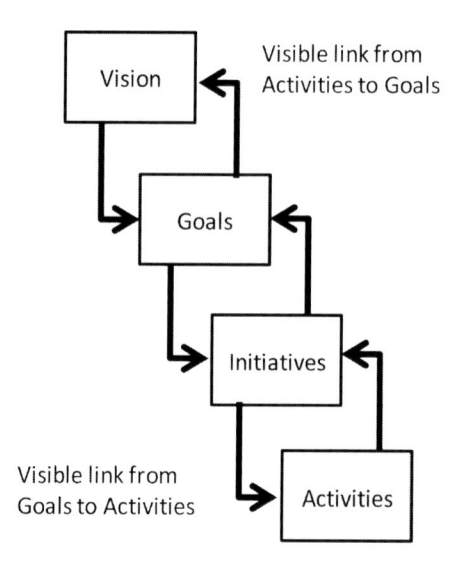

FIGURE 10 - THE INTERRELATIONSHIP OF THE MODEL'S COMPONENTS

Since there will be multiple initiatives supporting a goal and multiple activities supporting each initiative, you need to be careful since you cannot do everything at once. For that reason, you need to prioritize the work. Select three or four initiatives (those with the highest priority) and work on those first. As one is completed, you can then move on to the next. This helps to keep you focused and does not allow the process to get overwhelming.

There are some additional parts of the model that are also important. They are linked to the individual activities as shown in Figure 11.

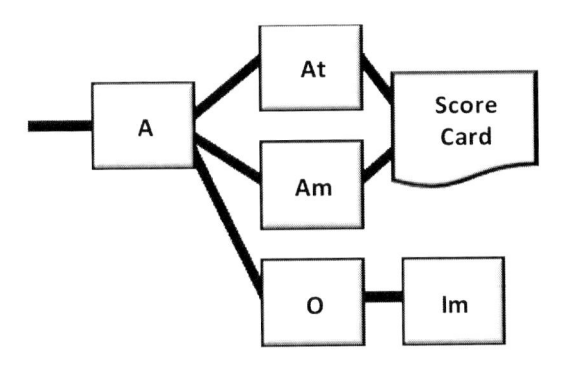

FIGURE 11 - ADDITIONAL COMPONENTS

In the diagram, At and Am represent the measurement parts of the model. There are two because you need to set initiative targets (At) and track the actual performance and completion of the activities (Am). You need both because even though you want to complete the initiatives, you need to complete the activities to make it happen. Failure to measure both is often the cause of initiative failure. Additionally, you need to examine the initiatives to make sure they are aligned with and driving the goals.

The last measurement section of the Goal Achievement Model is the scorecard. Many organizations create a composite scorecard so senior management can be brought up-to-date and track the effort's progress on one single page. The scorecard helps tie things together at a high level.

The other two blocks on this segment of the diagram stand for outcomes (O) and impacts (Im). Everything you or your organization does – especially within the change effort – has outcomes and impacts. These need to be positive for all involved and cannot be ignored. We will discuss them further in Chapter 9.

There is one more part of the Goal Achievement Model that cannot be left out. All activities resulting from your initiatives have one common characteristic – they are driven by one or more of the eight elements of change. For example, if one of your initiatives is to develop and deploy a machinery condition monitoring program, the activities will be tied to one or more of the eight elements. Table 1 attempts to place this into perspective.

INITIATIVE - DEVELOP AND DEPLOY A MACHINERY CONDITION MONITORING PROGRAM	
Activities	Link to the Eight Elements of Change
Develop and plan for implementation	Leadership
Detailing how the work will be performed	Work Process
Staffing	Structure
Training of the employees involved	Group Learning
Identifying and providing the correct tools	Technology
Informing the organization of the new process	Communication
Obtaining production buy-in and support	Interrelationships
Tracking and reinforcing the effort	Rewards

TABLE 1 - HOW THE EIGHT ELEMENTS OF CHANGE FIT THE GOAL ACHIEVEMENT MODEL

This is just a simple example. The problem arises when other initiatives also have ties to the same elements and possibly overlap. For this reason, a tracking tool such as Microsoft Access or Excel® should be used for monitoring and tracking purposes.

The following chapters address the elements of the model individually and explain how they are used to employ the Goal Achievement Model in an effective and efficient fashion.

Things to Think About & Things to Do

1. Select one or two goals with which you have had involvement.
    a. Was there a model in existence that enabled linking the goals to the vision?
    b. If not, what were the disconnects?
    c. How could issues created by the disconnected parts be improved?

2. Review the goal achievement process followed by your organization and compare it against the value proposition delivered by the Goal Achievement Model. Can you see the added value?

Vision and Goals

Vision and goals are the first two elements of the Goal Achievement Model. Because they are highly strategic and long term, there is not much interaction with the organization in their development. They are typically developed by the senior management team.

There should be only one primary vision that clearly depicts what senior management wishes the firm to achieve. As stated earlier, the vision needs to be clearly understood by all or you risk conflicting efforts as different parts of the organization try to accomplish what they believe the vision means.

A question often comes up, "Can we have a vision for the reliability maintenance organization that defines what we wish to achieve?" The answer is "yes," but with a qualification. That qualification is the vision for the reliability maintenance organization MUST support the vision of the company. Without this connection, you can only imagine the result – conflicts, problems, rework and more. The problem a conflicting vision creates is bad enough, but the rework will seriously undermine your credibility and cause problems before the actual work has begun.

A vision is also all-encompassing, addressing itself to a company wide effort. This means all departments in the organization are working to accomplish their part of the grand plan. These parts are the goals.

Goals are also strategic in nature and consequently are also developed by senior management. However, they are not set at the top level of the organization without input from the departments that will be charged with their completion.

In many organizations, goals are set yearly and not attended to until the next goal-setting or reporting period. The result of this causes several problems:

- They are put in a desk drawer only to be pulled out at review time when you are required to update your manager. The results are no organizational focus and no improvement.

- They are not realistic and are in conflict with how things really are done on a day-to-day basis. This results in frustration and lack of future engagement.

- There are so many goals created that the likelihood of success is seriously reduced as the organization is overloaded.

Establishing realistic, achievable and prioritized goals is an important part of the Goal Achievement Model process, but far more important is their need to be the driving force for improvement and change. This need creates what we shall call the Rules for Goal Development.

1. Goals are strategic in nature and must clearly support the attainment of the vision.

2. Goals need to be developed by management, but receive significant departmental input.

3. Goals are typically developed on a yearly basis and should show continuous improvement year to year.

4. You may develop as many goals as you need, but you must recognize that the organization can only work on a few at a time, so the goals need to be prioritized.

5. Goals may overlap departments or work groups and therefore require sound interrelationships so that overlaps can be identified and addressed.

6. Goals should be reviewed quarterly by a senior management oversight team with status reported and corrective action taken for those that are lagging.

7. A goal can be altered if there is sufficient reason – possibly something you learned that was not known when the original goal was developed. However, changes of this nature should be infrequent occurrences.

8. Reduction in the scope of a goal should be avoided.
9. Each goal requires a person who has sole accountability for its successful completion.
10. There should be individuals identified who are responsible for the actual work – this may not be the individual with sole accountability.
11. Communication, both quarterly and face-to-face with the organization, is critical so everyone understands what the organization is trying to accomplish and how the process is working.
12. Other communication tools, such as signage, billboards and newsletters, are important components so goals are visible on an ongoing basis.

An example is in order so that the high-level strategic nature of the vision and the supporting goals will be clear. Suppose the organization's vision is as follows:

> To operate the facility in a safe, environmentally-sound and reliable fashion supplying our products to the marketplace in an optimal manner.

This is clearly a multi-departmental vision. For the reliability maintenance organization, what would be the typical goals to support a vision of this nature? Here are a few:

1. Develop and implement a reliability-focused work process supporting optimal manufacturing by production.
2. Eliminate reactive repairs by identifying failure causes and implementing corrective action before the failure is allowed to become serious.
3. Create and implement a planning and scheduling process to optimize workforce productivity.

As you can see, these are high-level goals and do not have specific details attached that a group could address. The specifics are developed in the initiative and activity sections of the model, which are covered in the next two chapters.

Things to Think About & Things to Do

1. Does your organization have a vision for the future? What is it?

2. Is the vision well understood by everyone so there is a common picture of what the future holds?

    a. If asked, can a random sampling of the organization all relate the same vision?

3. List the reliability and maintenance goals that support the vision.

    a. Are they prioritized or are you expected to do all of them at the same time?

    b. If the latter is the case, what do you think will be the level of success?

4. Review your goals against the Rules for Goal Deployment. Do they fit? If not, then why?

5. How well does your goal development effort work? Could there be improvements?

Initiatives

The next element of the Goal Achievement Model is initiatives. With initiatives, we are no longer in the area where the efforts are defined by senior management. Initiatives are determined within middle management and only validated by upper management to make certain they directly support the established goals.

There is often confusion between goals and initiatives and the terms are often used interchangeably. However, in order for the model to work properly, there needs to be a clear differentiation between the two terms and each needs to be used correctly.

As you have learned, goals are "high level" and very strategic in nature. You know you are working with goals when what you identify clearly requires more detail before you can assign it for development and execution. For example, create a reliability program, develop a program to support the safety efforts of the firm, or create an optimized production process are all goals because they are strategic, broad and far-reaching. Additionally, there is more detail required before action can be taken. Further, as a manager, you would not assign something this nebulous and expect the final effort to resemble your thoughts about a desired outcome. Goals require more detail and that is where the initiatives come into play.

Initiatives are far more specific and definitive than goals. They provide a broad definition of the effort you want put forth to achieve the goal of which they are a part.

Initiatives are developed by the middle management team and subject matter experts with oversight from the senior leadership team. If you are wise, you may also solicit input from the technicians and mechanics to add value and obtain buy-in. As you can see in Figure 12, just as with goals, there can be more than one initiative for each goal.

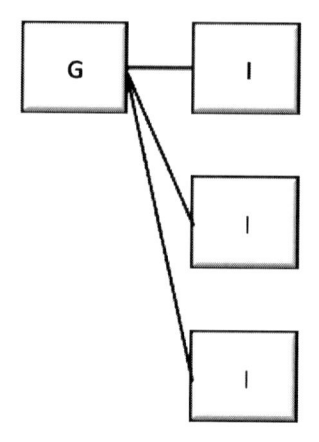

FIGURE 12 - MULTIPLE INITIATIVES FOR EACH GOAL

Again, just like with goals, the number of initiatives needs to be managed through a prioritization process simply because the organization cannot successfully work on a vast array of initiatives at the same time.

There is another aspect related to the successful attainment of your initiatives that addresses an organization's comfort zone. It is understood that the changes being implemented will take the majority of the organization's population out of the zone of comfort. An example would be switching the organizational focus from reactive to predictive maintenance. While everyone may understand at some level that the change is needed, working outside your comfort zone – individually or collectively – can cause problems and serious discomfort for those involved. The change is often contrary to the existing culture, the value system, the role models, as well as the existing rites and rituals. In other words, the change will have an enormous impact on the culture – the foundation of organizational behavior. When this happens, the organization is going to resist. Many managers believe that resistance is something to overcome. This is not true! Resistance must be understood and addressed so that moving outside of the organization's comfort zone is attainable. To be able to address resistance, you need to be able to recognize its many forms. Figure 13 depicts a resistance model called a quad diagram.

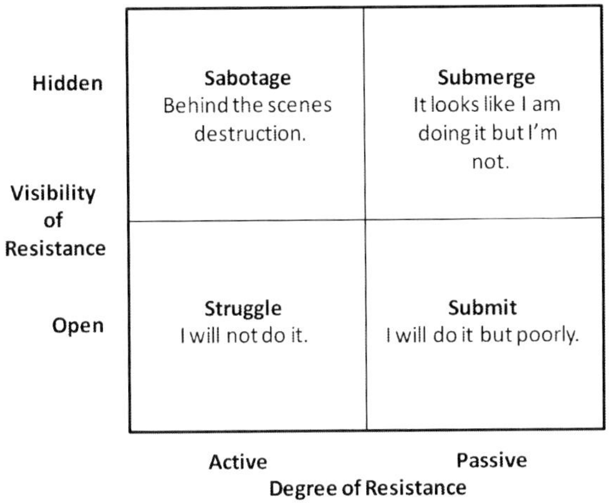

	Active	Passive
Hidden	**Sabotage** Behind the scenes destruction.	**Submerge** It looks like I am doing it but I'm not.
Open	**Struggle** I will not do it.	**Submit** I will do it but poorly.

Visibility of Resistance (vertical axis) — Degree of Resistance (horizontal axis)

FIGURE 13 - RESISTANCE QUAD DIAGRAM

Reprinted with permission from Industrial Press, Inc.

The diagram is self explanatory – resistance can be hidden or open, as well as active or passive. This provides you with four different possible ways in which the organization can resist. In each case, you need to first recognize that resistance is taking place and then figure out why, so the issue can be mitigated. Often, the simplest way to achieve this is to ask, why? This indicates that you are aware of the problem and shows willingness to try to remedy the situation. This, or other similar approaches, work well in three of the four scenarios. Things are different when it comes to sabotage because in this case, resistance is manifesting itself as destruction of company assets, resources, or processes. While this form of resistance also requires mitigation, the approach needs to be severe to indicate it is not going to be an accepted mode of performance.

Just as with goals, initiatives need review, but with greater frequency. The status of the initiatives initially should be reviewed weekly by an oversight team to ensure that work is on track. As things start getting accomplished, the frequency can be extended.

With your initiatives established, the ground work is almost set for the change effort to be put into place. However, we still have not discussed the details that enable you to accomplish the initiatives that have been developed. We will discuss this phase in the next chapter on activities.

Things to Think About & Things to Do

1. Take a few of the reliability and maintenance goals you listed in Chapter 5.

    a. Do they have defined initiatives linked to them? If so, list them. If not, why not?

    b. If there are no linked initiatives, what do you think will be the likelihood of successful goal achievement?

    c. If there are initiatives associated with the goals, do they fit the definition?

    d. Are your initiatives prioritized?

2. As goals and initiatives are implemented, they often take people within the organization out of their comfort zone.

    a. Do you have a method to recognize the resistance that results from this type of change?

    b. What is it?

Activities

Activities are the detailed steps required to achieve the initiatives. For many initiatives, there will be a large number of associated activities. Many can begin as soon as the initiative is set, some need other activities to be completed first and still others can be completed in parallel. It sounds a little like a Gantt chart and, in fact, that is exactly what we are discussing. The sequence of the activities can't really be determined until they are all identified. This takes work and time. There are rules that, if followed, will help you develop and sequence the activities. They are:

1. A cross-sectional interdepartmental team will be better at developing the activity list as opposed to doing it on your own. This approach provides a broader focus and allows for multiple perspectives. Handling this as a team also promotes understanding and buy-in for the overall effort.

2. There needs to be a clear linkage between the activities, the initiatives, the goals and ultimately, the vision. If there is not, quite possibly you are working on the wrong activities.

3. Not all activities will be identified at the onset. Many will emerge as your team works through the activity identification process and recognizes additional requirements.

4. You can't do all the activities at once, even if there are many that can all start immediately. Prioritization is the key.

5. Many activities depend on the completion of others before they can begin. Identifying these early and linking them to their predecessors will avoid false starts.

6. You need to have objective oversight in place to assure that nothing is missed during the activity development effort. The oversight function also needs to be tasked with keeping the effort within scope.

7. Activities will complete at different times and the entire set needs to be tracked on an ongoing basis. This enables everyone to see the status of each item and take corrective action as needed for those that are lagging.

As you develop your activity list for each initiative, pay careful attention to the eight elements of change. Every activity will be tied to one or more of the elements. Also for each activity, you need to consider how each of the elements is addressed and make sure that none are missed. Missing the elements and failing to see how they fit with the activities will head you down the path of failure.

Let's see how this concept works through an example.

Vision: Set by the senior leadership team

Goal: Establish a reliability-focused maintenance effort

Initiative: Provide accurate asset history within the computerized maintenance management system (CMMS)

Activity: Conduct a physical walk down of all assets and gather correct nameplate data for entry into the CMMS

How do the eight elements of change fit this activity?

Leadership: They support the effort with resources, funds and oversight.

Work Process: This element defines how the work will be accomplished.

Structure: A team (outside of the day-to-day effort) will be created for this purpose.

Group Learning: The process will be continually improved as it progresses and things are learned along the way.

Technology: The CMMS will need a method of data entry and standard formatting, among other things.

Communication:	There needs to be communication throughout the organization so everyone understands what is taking place and why. Communication efforts may be able to add value.
Interrelationships:	Since the team will be walking down the assets, production will need to be involved so they can help the team locate the assets and, if needed, make them available.
Rewards:	Accurate database information for future reliability-based decisions has numerous benefits and rewards.

Once the activities are developed, individuals and teams need to be assigned the work with stated completion dates and a description of the expected outcome.

- **Assignment** – This is a critical requirement for success. Assignment of activity responsibility should be made to teams or individuals who can reasonably be expected to complete the work. Additionally, if a team assignment is made, there needs to be a single member of the team with overall responsibility. Often, the key players in your organization are already very busy and may not have the time to take on additional work. If you prefer them to take on these activities, they need to have someone else pick up their current job duties. The old adage, "you should do this job along with what you are already doing," is a key to failure for two reasons. First, the individual is most likely fully engaged and additional work is not going to be easily added to their workload. Second, and even more important, is the person is most likely engaged in task-related work and what we are talking about here is strategic. Remember, tactics and strategic work do not easily coexist.

- **Timing** – The due dates for activities should be attainable. Manager's who say, "I want this yesterday" are unrealistic and are setting the effort up for failure. Also assigning a date far in the future is not a practical approach because other things will get in the way and the activity will only be addressed as the completion date nears.

- **Outcomes** – While the actual outcome will be the result of the effort on the collective activities, a general idea of what is expected should be provided. This can be used as a guide to make certain that the activity is within the scope.
- **Fit** – Since the activity is only one of many, it is important that those assigned understand how what they are doing fits the initiative, goal and vision. This is important so everyone sees how they are contributing, as well as makes certain that the activity or activities on which they are working are in sync with the others in progress.

With all of the initiatives and activities underway, a tracking tool is needed. The form that I suggest is shown in Figure 14.

Goal Achievement Model Form						
Vision:						
Goal:						
ID# / Initiative Description:						
ID#	Activity Description	Activity Status	Assigned To	Due Date	Perc't Complete	Date Completed

FIGURE 14 - THE GOAL ACHIEVEMENT MODEL TRACKING FORM

This form is just an example. There are many creative ways to monitor the initiative/activity status and I leave the development to the reader. However, I do suggest that all the columns shown be included. Here are some additional thoughts:
- Since the vision and goal generate multiple initiatives and activities, there is no need for columns for these parts because it would just become repetitive. Showing them once is sufficient.

- The initiatives and activities need a numbering system associated with them for tracking purposes.

- A status column is needed for tracking purposes since these forms will be used in the oversight review sessions. This will be covered in Chapter 11 on sustainability. This also holds true for the Percentage Complete and Due Date columns.

- The Assigned To column should indicate the individual who has sole responsibility, even if the assignment was made to a team.

- The completion date is also important so the organization knows when the activity was completed and if it was completed by the due date.

Last but not least, remember to reference the activities to the eight elements of change. Make sure the work on each activity addresses (if needed) each of the elements. Failure to do so could cause you problems down the road.

Things to Think About & Things to Do

1. Take a few of the reliability and maintenance initiatives you listed in Chapter 6.

    a. Do they have defined activities linked to them? If so, list them. If not, why not?

    b. If not, what do you think will be the likelihood of successful goal achievement?

    c. If there are activities associated with the initiatives, do they fit the definition?

    d. Are your activities sequenced and prioritized?

2. Review several of your initiatives with their associated activities to determine if the eight elements of change are addressed. If there are missing elements, consider the impact on successful goal, initiative and activity achievements.

3. Select an activity and check to make certain your process addresses assignment, timing, defining expected outcomes and fit.

Measurement | 8

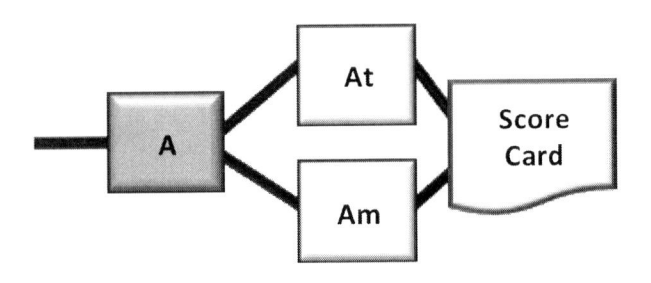

FIGURE 15 - MEASUREMENT

To this point, we briefly discussed measures and noted that initiatives and activities need to be tracked on a rather frequent basis. This ensures that they are in progress and that the progress is proceeding in a continuous fashion. We have all experienced efforts that were tracked with an extended duration between review sessions. It seems that in these cases, very little gets accomplished until just before the review meeting. At this point, there is a flurry of activity so those who have responsibility for the effort have something to report. This is a terrible way to approach a change effort. Things are not done with thought and planning, they are just done to stay out of trouble. Frequent reviews keep the work proceeding smoothly, show commitment and indicate to all concerned the importance of the effort.

There are two types of measures in the Goal Achievement Model. They are referred to as initiative targets (At) and activity measures (Am). The initiative targets are the milestones you set for getting the initiative developed and deployed. The activity measures are the due dates established for the completion of each specific activity. As you can probably see, completion of the activity measures support completion of the initiative target.

For those of you familiar with Gantt charts, the initiative target and activity measures are displayed in Figure 16.

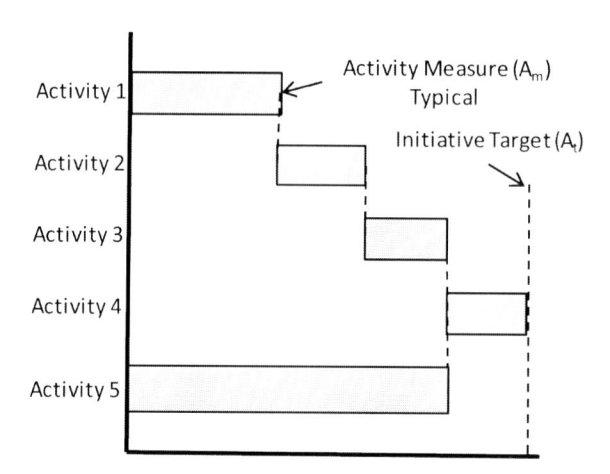

FIGURE 16 - INITIATIVE WITH INITIATIVE TARGET AND ACTIVITY MEASURES

There are a great many different measurements used in the reliability maintenance business, often called key performance indicators or KPIs for short. These have nothing to do with the Goal Achievement Model. They track overall performance in areas such as schedule compliance, mean time between failure and many others. The measures we are discussing have one purpose and one purpose only – to measure if activities and their related initiatives are being completed as planned.

For example, if the initiative was to reduce the number of emergency work orders, activities that were measured might include the establishment of an emergency job approval process, the development and deployment of a post job analysis process and others. But as you can see, the activity measures track the work performed to complete the initiative.

As previously mentioned, a monthly review of the initiatives by the oversight team is a sound practice. However, to keep the activities progressing smoothly towards their completion dates, a middle management supervisory review is needed on a much more frequent basis. This review does not need to be a formal meeting, but it does require that activity progress is checked and corrective action taken for those that are lagging behind their due dates.

There is also a section of the model as shown in Figure 17 where the initiative targets, as well as the work that was completed for that initiative, is checked against the goal to make certain the work being performed is in alignment. Remember, we want the organization to see how what they are doing at the initiative and activity levels relate to the established goal. This effort validates that linkage.

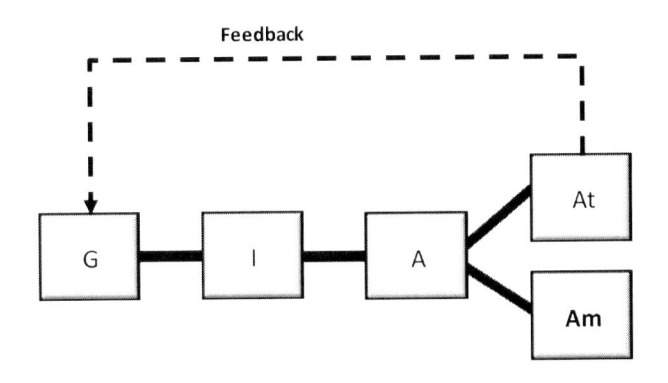

FIGURE 17 - LINKAGE INITIATIVE TARGETS TO THE GOALS

We also do not want to forget the concept of a scorecard. This is nothing more than a summary of all the goals and initiatives formatted in a manner that can be presented to the senior management oversight team. This should be a one- or two-page report that you can develop for this purpose. After all, we know how management teams typically don't want a report with a lot of pages to sort through in order to find out the status of the effort.

Last but not least – a word of caution.

All too often when you start to talk about measurement, the management team immediately begins to address the high-level measures they are used to seeing in their typical reports. While these types of measures are very important, this is not what the initiative targets and activity measures are meant to address. They are much more specific, detailed and focused. Failure to use these measures properly defeats the purpose and functioning of the model.

Things to Think About & Things to Do

1. Do you have a formal process to track and review the status of the initiatives and activities?

    a. Is it separate from the established KPIs?

    b. If not, why?

2. What is the frequency of the review process?

    a. Is it sufficient to keep the effort on track in a continuous fashion?

3. Is there an oversight function that conducts the review and ensures there is corrective action where required?

Outcomes and Impacts

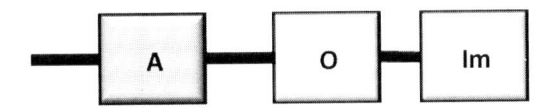

FIGURE 18 - OUTCOMES AND IMPACTS FROM ACTIVITIES

Outcomes and impacts are the last two components of the Goal Achievement Model. Every initiative and their associated activities carry with them outcomes and impacts.

Outcomes are the results that emerge from the things you do within the context of the change effort. Everything has an outcome; some have more than one. By themselves, outcomes are just events, but when coupled with impacts, the work begins.

Impacts are the effects that the outcomes create. They can be positive or negative for you or for others. Obviously, we wish to avoid negative outcomes at all costs, but that is not always necessarily the case. Negative impacts are real to those who are affected. However, while those impacted may initially feel negatively, the outcome still may be in the best interest of the organization. The reason for this is those who feel the negative impact may be judging it from the viewpoint of the existing culture. I would suspect a team of maintenance firefighters may view a planning and scheduling process with the elimination of emergency jobs as a negative impact when, in fact, that is far from the case.

There are also impacts that, even in the context of the new culture, have the potential of being truly negative. In these cases, there needs to be some mitigation effort to reverse a negative impact into one that is as positive as possible.

In addition to the above two scenarios, there is one other. The timing of the outcome may be the thing that is causing the negative impact, not the initiative and activity themselves. An example of this might be deploying a new cost control system right before a major plant outage. In this case, the new system may be just what was needed, but the timing for deployment brings with it a negative impact. Timing issues are often far easier to resolve than perception issues by simply changing (if possible) the time frame of the activity.

Failure to address the mitigation of negative impacts is going to lead to problems with whatever it is you are trying to implement. Therefore, you need a process that will enable you to identify negative impacts and take the needed correct mitigation action. This can be handled by the use of the Outcome/Impact Corrective Action Worksheet shown in Figure 19.

Outcome / Impact Corrective Action Worksheet			
Initiative:			
Activity:			
Expected Outcome:			
Impact (if negative):		On You	On Others:
Negative Impact Based On:	Perception		
	Actual Result		
	Timing		
Mitigation Required:			
Assigned To:		Completion Date:	
Results:			
Date Closed:		Comment:	

FIGURE 19 - OUTCOME/IMPACT CORRECTIVE ACTION WORKSHEET

This worksheet is self explanatory. Its sole purpose is to force the organization to identify and confront negative impacts in order to make the change process much smoother.

It is a fact that not every perceived negative impact needs to be mitigated. Some simply must get implemented even though there are those in the organization that are unhappy. Once again, the eight elements of change can help you over this hurdle.

- Leadership needs to visibly lead the effort and be available to explain what is taking place and why.
- Work processes need to be in place before the change so everyone can see a new and clear path.
- Structure, where necessary, needs to be created to support the effort.
- Technology needs to be provided to support the work process. This is often accomplished within the computerized maintenance management system (CMMS) or other forms of electronic software.
- Group learning through the training process should be provided before the initiative is deployed. The other aspects of group learning, feedback and corrective action, may also be in order.
- Communication about what is taking place is crucial or the cultural infrastructure will fill the void with misinformation, thus making your job all the more difficult.
- Interrelationships, especially those built on mutual trust and respect, will go a long way towards having your mitigation strategy accepted.
- Rewards or other benefits resulting from the change effort need to be presented, showing the inherent value and reversing negative opinion.

While outcomes and impacts are at the tail end of the Goal Achievement Model, they are not to be overlooked. It is fine to develop and deploy goals, initiatives and activities, but without understanding and acceptance, problems will get in your way.

Things to Think About & Things to Do

1. Does your organization take outcomes and impacts into consideration as part of the change efforts they deploy?
    a. If not, identify some of the problems this can cause.
    b. If they were part of the effort, how did this help to mitigate negative impacts?

2. Think about an initiative whose outcome was successful, but was perceived as a negative impact on the organization.
    a. What was done to mitigate the negative impact?
    b. How well did this help the effort?
    c. If nothing was done, what was the result of this decision?

An Example of How It Works

Now that we have examined the cultural and strategic elements of change along with the elements of the Goal Achievement Model, it is time for an example to illustrate how all of the parts fit together. The example has one additional purpose and that is to provide you with a model that can be replicated as you create your own goal model.

First of all, the vision should have already been established by the senior leadership team. Without a vision, the effort cannot proceed since you can't strive for an ideal future state if one has not been defined. Typical visions usually talk about being number one at whatever the company produces. For our example, let's assume a simplified vision for your organization was established as: We will be the number one producer of product "X" and deliver it to our customers in a safe, reliable and environmentally-sound manner.

Using the Goal Achievement Model, the next step is to develop a series of goals that support the vision. There will be several goals addressing various functions within the firm since each organizational function needs goals if the expected vision is to be achieved. For our example, we will limit the discussion to the goal of reliability. Yes, there may be additional goals within the maintenance and reliability arena, but for now we are just going to focus on one. Therefore, our goal statement related to reliability is: Develop and deploy efforts that will provide highly reliable equipment and manufacturing processes for optimal product delivery.

With the vision and goal set in place, the real work begins. To support the goal, we are going to require that many initiatives be developed by the management team or teams along with subject matter expertise.

The initiatives for our example are as follows:
1. Develop and implement a preventive maintenance program;
2. Develop and implement predictive technologies;
3. Create and implement a planning and scheduling process;
4. Assess and upgrade the technical skills of the maintenance mechanics;
5. Improve the integrity of the asset data promoting reliability-based decision making.

Of note is the fact that these are not all the initiatives that will be created, but they provide a good sampling for our example. The first thing you probably recognized is you can't do all of the initiatives at once. Therefore, as we discussed in the chapter on initiatives, we need to prioritize the list. Let's assume we could conceivably work on three of these initiatives with the remainder waiting on the priority list for completion of the higher priority items.

Since our example organization is highly reactive — they are the best firefighters in the business — and since our goal is to be reliable, this focus needs to change. Therefore, we shall select item numbers 1, 2 and 3 above as our priority initiatives.

Next are the activities. Since the detailed development of this phase of the Goal Achievement Model will be similar for each initiative, we will just take one and build it out.

One of the major differences between a highly reactive organization and one that is reliability-focused is the inclusion of a detailed and rigidly-enforced planning and scheduling process. The reason is because a process of this nature that is both effective and efficient seldom exists in a highly reactive work environment.

What follows is an abbreviated list of the large number of activities that would be generated in this process.

INITIATIVE:	ACTIVITIES SUPPORTING THIS INITIATIVE:
Create and implement a planning and scheduling process.	1. Develop the work process 2. Obtain planners and a scheduler – hiring 3. Train planners and the scheduler 4. Assure the process is in sync with the CMMS functionality 5. Communicate the change to the organization 6. Obtain process buy-in from production 7. Develop measurement KPIs 8. Engage leadership to show continuous support *There are more, but I am sure you get the idea.*

If you look carefully, you may notice something familiar about the activities listed; each can be tied directly to one of the eight elements of change. This is something to remember as you develop your activities. You need to evaluate the activities and make certain the eight elements of change are addressed. Don't forget what you learned earlier about the results of missing one or more of the elements and therefore reducing the collective value they provide.

Once the activity list is developed, it needs to be prioritized. You also need to take time as part of the prioritization process to recognize dependencies that will also help with the prioritization process. For example, you can't train your planners until you have hired them. This may seem obvious, but there are less apparent dependencies that will make the effort easier once they are recognized.

The next step in the activity phase is determining who will do the work and when it needs to be completed. This part also requires careful consideration because everyone is already busy and you are, in essence, adding work to their already busy schedule.

You are making progress, but you are still not done! Don't forget the review of the outcomes and impacts and the need to try to mitigate those that are negative in nature – for you or for others.

Let's suppose that the best mechanics are assigned to production in order to handle day-to-day emergency issues. Further, let's suppose that these mechanics, at least a few of them, are the ones you wish to make planners. Do you think the outcome of the hiring process is going to have a positive impact on production as you pull their key emergency responders? Definitely not! This is where negative impact mitigation comes into play. You know that with improved reliability and a rigid planning and scheduling process the emergencies will be virtually eliminated, removing the need for emergency responders. The problem is that production doesn't know this and the existing culture does not believe it. Therefore, as your reliability change effort is deployed, you need a short-term fix to address the perceived negative impact. The answer may be to assign another mechanic temporarily to the job. Of course production is going to want their former mechanics back on the job, but this may serve to mitigate resistance to the planning and scheduling initiative.

This is how the Goal Achievement Model works. Naturally, you will need to provide an ongoing status for the effort and for this I refer you back to Chapter 8.

The Goal Achievement Model is a value-added process if used correctly. It provides focus and establishes a clear connection between each and every activity and the overall vision for the organization.

Things to Think About Things to Do

1. Take the vision, goals, initiatives and activities used in prior exercises and develop a full blown Goal Achievement Model. This will give you practice using the process. Don't forget the measures and the outcomes and impacts. If pieces of the process are missing, create them on your own. The idea is to gain some experience using the model. Hopefully, you will see the value and use your example to demonstrate it to your management team.

Sustainability

The Goal Achievement Model process is continuous. Initiatives and their related activities are completed and others are added and the process goes on. However, as much as we would like this effort and the associated benefits it provides to be self perpetuating, that is not the case. For a whole host of reasons, people get distracted by other business requirements, they change jobs, or real emergencies crop up that take them away from their focused efforts on the change initiative.

Since we know that change is a process with no real end, how do you maintain focus over the long term? The answer is once again provided by the eight elements of change – leadership, work process, structure, group learning, technology, communication, interrelationships and rewards.

- It is the leadership's responsibility to see to it that the effort is not abandoned. One way to accomplish this is to establish a review board that meets frequently to review the status of the active initiatives and activities. This oversight team should have a member of the senior leadership team as the chair with other members serving on the committee. While it won't always be possible to review every item at every review meeting, a schedule should be established so over a set time period all items are discussed. This type of effort shows continued support and allows for timely corrective action for those efforts that are lagging.
- Work process is the key to successful sustainability. Having review board meetings and an established, well documented and widely understood process goes a long way to making certain that the ef-

fort supported by the Goal Achievement Model does not fall off the organization's radar.

- Structure and process go hand-in-hand. The review board and a dedicated group of individuals focused on the effort will have far-reaching impact on sustaining the long-term effort.

- Group learning is also important. The process of change is non-linear. In other words, you learn as you go using feedback and corrective action to add to the collective knowledge base and make the effort in the future even better. Failure to recognize the non-linearity of the process will lead to stagnation since the process will never be improved.

- Technology, or the system tools you have at your disposal, enables a wide-range of data management possibilities supporting the long-term effort.

- Communication is also a critical factor. Since the change effort will affect everyone in some way, they need to know on an ongoing basis what is happening and what is planned for their future. This will provide significant help in keeping everyone engaged, while at the same time reducing the negative impact of the cultural infrastructure.

- Interrelationships also play an important part. Since change in an organization does not happen in a vacuum, there needs to be strong positive relations across departmental boundaries. After all, how could you sustain any multi-departmental effort if the members are not getting along?

- Rewards, the eighth element of change, are what reinforces the work being done. There are all forms of reinforcement, but the important piece of the puzzle is that reinforcement needs to be developed and employed to support the effort over the long term. Short-term reinforcement that winds down over time will not provide the sustaining force required.

There is one more sustainability element for consideration. Even if everything is working like clockwork, a third-party audit of the overall effort on a periodic basis will uncover areas that are experiencing problems or where improvements can be made. By third-party, I mean just that. Individuals in the organization that understand what is taking place, but have no day-to-day involvement, can be employed over a short period of time to conduct the audit and make recommendations for improvement.

Things to Think About & Things to Do

1. Identify several initiatives in which you have been involved that added value to the organization.

    a. Was a sustaining process employed to keep the effort alive over time?

    b. If so, what was it?

    c. If not, then what should have been done so it was sustained?

The Beginning

On the surface, the Goal Achievement Model process seems so simple. Set your vision, establish goals, create the supporting initiatives and activities, examine the outcomes and impacts, and create a sustainability process. However, if this effort was so simple, why do about 80% of the change initiatives fail? There are many answers to this question, many of which are specific to the company involved in the change effort. Nevertheless, one overriding reason is the process described in this book was not completely followed. The result of this is a breakdown within the process and the ultimate failure to achieve the goals and vision. But it doesn't have to be that way! Use this book, the concepts, diagrams, the form and the example to change the way you address the process of change. Do this and I promise that you will be pleasantly surprised with the result.

Feel free to contact me with questions and the results of Things to Think About/Things to Do. I am interested in your experiences, problems and successful outcomes. All information will be held in strictest confidence.

Steve Thomas
changemgt999@yahoo.com

BIBLIOGRAPHY

Schein, Edgar H. *Organizational Culture and Leadership,2e.* San Francisco: Jossey Bass, 1992.

Thomas, Stephen J. *Successfully Managing Change in Organizations: A User's Guide.* New York: Industrial Press, 2001.

Thomas, Stephen J. *Improving Maintenance & Reliability Through Cultural Change.* New York: Industrial Press, 2005.

Thomas, Stephen J. *Improving Reliability and Maintenance from Within: How to Be an Effective Internal Consultant.* New York: Industrial Press, 2007.

ABOUT THE AUTHOR

Steve Thomas has 40 years of experience working in the petrochemical industry. During this time, through personal involvement at all levels of the maintenance and reliability work process, he has gained vast experience in all phases of the business. Coupled with a B.S. in Electrical Engineering from Drexel University and M.S. degrees in both Systems Engineering and Organizational Dynamics from the University of Pennsylvania, this experience has enabled him to add significant value to the many projects on which he has worked. In addition, he has published seven books on change management and other subjects through Industrial Press, Inc, and Reliabilityweb.com. He has also presented training classes on his material in the US, Canada and South America.

About Reliabilityweb.com

Created in 1999, Reliabilityweb.com provides educational information and peer-to-peer networking opportunities that enable safe and effective maintenance reliability and asset management for organizations around the world.

Activities include:

Reliabilityweb.com (www.reliabilityweb.com) includes educational articles, tips, video presentations, an industry event calendar and industry news. Updates are available through free email subscriptions and RSS feeds. **Confiabilidad.net** is a mirror site that is available in Spanish at www.confiabilidad.net

Uptime Magazine (www.uptimemagazine.com) is a bi-monthly magazine launched in 2005 that is highly prized by the maintenance reliability and asset management community. Editions are obtainable in print, online, digital, Kindle and through the iPad/iPhone app.

Reliability Performance Institute Conferences and Training Events (www.maintenanceconference.com) offer events that range from unique, focused-training workshops and seminars to small focused conferences to large industry-wide events, including the International Maintenance Conference, now in its 26th year.

MRO-Zone Bookstore (www.mro-zone.com) is an online bookstore offering a maintenance reliability and asset management focused library of books, DVDs and CDs published by Reliabilityweb.com and other leading publishers, such as Industrial Press, McGraw-Hill, CRC Press and more.

Association for Maintenance Professionals (www.maintenance.org) is a member organization and online community that encourages professional development and certification and supports information exchange and learning with 10,000+ members worldwide.

A Word About Social Good

Reliabilityweb.com is mission driven to deliver value and social good to the maintenance reliability and asset management communities. *Doing good work and making profit is not inconsistent*, and as a result of Reliabilityweb.com's mission-driven focus, financial stability and success has been the outcome. Over the past 12 years, Reliabilityweb.com's positive contributions and commitment to the maintenance reliability and asset management communities are unmatched.

Other causes Reliabilityweb.com has financially contributed to include industry associations, such as SMRP, AFE, STLE, ASME and ASTM, and community charities, including the Salvation Army, American Red Cross, Wounded Warrior Project, Paralyzed Veterans of America and the Autism Society of America. In addition, we are proud supporters of our U.S. Troops and first responders who protect our freedoms and way of life. That is only possible by being a for-profit company that pays taxes.

I hope you will get involved with and explore the many resources that are available to you through the Reliabilityweb.com network.

Warmest regards,
Terrence O'Hanlon
CEO, Reliabilityweb.com